Fresh Manna

from God

Love letters inspired
by the Holy Spirit

Verse by Kay Bonnell
Photographs by Dana Kay Bonnell

WestBow Press books may be ordered through booksellers or by contacting:

WestBow Press
A Division of Thomas Nelson & Zondervan
1663 Liberty Drive
Bloomington, IN 47403
www.westbowpress.com
1 (866) 928-1240

Because of the dynamic nature of the Internet, any web addresses or links contained in this book may have changed since publication and may no longer be valid. The views expressed in this work are solely those of the author and do not necessarily reflect the views of the publisher, and the publisher hereby disclaims any responsibility for them.

ISBN: 978-1-4908-2300-3 (sc)
ISBN: 978-1-4908-2301-0 (e)

Library of Congress Control Number: 2014900904

Printed in the United States of America.

WestBow Press rev. date: 02/21/2014

I dedicate *Fresh Manna from God* to the Holy Spirit. I knew I could rely on Him, for without His faithfulness this book would have been impossible.

"My sheep hear my voice, and I know them, and they follow me." John 10:27

Why do you feel alone?

Can you not see me? Can you not hear me?

I am here.

I am as close by as the air surrounding you.

I am as close as the breeze that touches your face;

as the sun ray that warms your body;

as close as the sound of the waves that brush the shore.

I am not a distant God who sits on high in judgement.

I am inside you;

I am the joy that escapes;

I am the smile that comes for no reason;

I am hope that rises unbidden.

You are not alone;

you never have been;

you never will be.

Father God

Faith

is the key

that unlocks the

treasures

that lie in store

for those who

believe.

Father God

There will be seasons
in your life filled with trials.

Do not lose hope;
do not falter under the weight of adversity.

Look at me;
keep your eyes on me and not on the problem.

Always seek me first,
not as your last resort.

I always have the answer;

I am the answer.

Call out and I will hear;
ask and I will show you the way.

Father God

Child,

why do you suppress the joy that is within you?

Leap and sing!

Let the angels hear!

Clash the cymbals, blow the trumpet, *rejoice* for your Lord has come!

Sing praises to His holy name.

Let *praise* and **thanksgiving** never leave your lips.

Prepare the way of the Lord; prepare for His *triumphant* return!

Father God

Do not fear growing old.

Wisdom, that which is prized above all things, comes with age.

The sage is to be sought out,
his words are to be a guide post to those who come behind.

Still seek me as you age;
I am your source of aid through all stages of life.

Why would I leave you when you are old?

Have I not spent many years with you?

Have you not come to know me for who I really am?

Would I leave you now when you need me the most?

The world may turn its back on you;
they are blind to the treasure they have in you.

Old age drops all pretenses.   I will never turn away.

Old age brings you face to face with eternity.

Realize that I am but a heartbeat away
and every angel in heaven awaits your coming.

There is nothing to fear; anticipate our reunion,

expect an everlasting welcome!

Father God

Absolute faith requires absolute trust.

Father God

A heart that has been mended feels no pain.

A heart that has been mended forgives and forgets.

I can mend your broken heart.

Through the tears and sorrow,

as you are able,

look at, relive, and experience once again the hurt;

then bit by bit release it to me.

Father God

Happiness

can never be found in this world.

True happiness,
a lifting of your spirit, soul,
and body is only found in me.

What the world offers is fleeting.

True contentment comes from knowing who I am and,
once you realize that,

you will know who you are.

Seek Godly wisdom,

walk in her light for she will show you true happiness,
a state of being that no earthly situation can alter.

Trust me in all things and

I will give you the desires of your heart.

Father God

*W*hat are you going to do?

*S*earch for me with all your

heart,

mind,

soul,

and strength;

then you will know.

Father God

I
can
and
will
do
everything
as
soon
as
you
believe
it.
Father God

*The darkness that surrounds you is thick,
do you see no way out?*

*Is your spirit within at a loss?
Are you desperate for help?
Is hope a thing of the past?*

*I have a lifeline for you. I am that faint
ray of light that you see in the midst of
the darkness.*

*Make no mistake, the light is becoming brighter,
darkness cannot stay when my light, my presence,
starts to overcome. There is hope in that light;
there is earth shaking, mountain moving
power in that light.*

*Keep your eyes on the light, do not look away.
Grasp it, hold on to it. Let it bring you through
the valley of pain and fear; the valley of anger,
disappointment, and death.*

*Trust in me; trust that I love you enough to bring
you through your darkness into a new day of light
and life.*

Father God

Fear is the means by which the Devil controls my people.

Fear is not from me;
it never has been,
it never will be.

I do not lead, guide, or direct by fear.

Love is my motivator;
love is the catalyst that moves mountains
in the lives of those who follow me.

Fear torments, love liberates.

Fear holds captive, love sets free.

Fear dominates, love releases.

Love sets no limits.

When my people live their lives motivated by love,
fear has no foothold.

Cast out fear! Live in love!

Father God

An offering made in faith opens the gates of heaven.

Father God

Forgiveness

is a seed that is planted in the heart.
It grows and multiplies as it is
watered and fed with love.

Forgiveness is essential;

for without it
nothing can be accomplished.

When my church forgives,
it opens the door to my being able to forgive them.

Repentance and forgiveness go hand in hand.

Seek a pure heart,

one that is free of wounds that only tie and bind.

Forgiveness toward others and yourself

frees my hand to move.

Father God

Come and feast at my table;

just come!

Father God

So many of my people,
my creation, my church,
ask at some point in their lives;

What is my purpose?

Why am I here?

I wait so anxiously for that day.

I wait for that day because this is my opportunity to tell them
the truth of their existence.

When they ask this question it means
they have come to the end of themselves,
finding that the world holds nothing for them.

Now they are ready to listen,
to hear in their hearts my answer.

You are here because I placed you here.

I need you;

I need you to spread my love,

my word, to all.

I need you to bring everyone to me.

I desire every created being to dwell with me forever.

Spread the truth to every ear that will listen.

Hold the hand of everyone who will embrace me and lead them into my presence.

Show them who I am.

Father God

Cast overboard
everything
you thought you could not
live without.

Father God

Peace

I give to you, not as the world
gives; my peace endures forever.
My peace is as a stone;
a rock unmovable, unshakeable,
unrelenting in my desire to help,
to deliver, to bring to
victory all that you aspire to.
Rely on me, cling to me, pursue me
with everything in you,
and where you find me,
my peace,
my serenity,
will fill you and make you whole.

Father God

The winds blow, the storm rages; your heart is breaking.

Hold back the flood, turn away the sorrows that threaten to drown you.

Reach for the life raft; reach for me.

In this violent storm of sorrow, grief, and pain

I am there. Reach out to me.

Call my name and I will reach out to you;
to embrace you, to enfold you in my mighty, sure arms;
to keep you from sinking, to hold you afloat until the sunrise.

I will hold you for as long as it takes.

Rest on me, lean on me, speak to me as you anguish.

Release it all to me

and I will fill those broken, empty places with hope.

I feel your tears on my cheek; they will remain there with me forever.

Father God

Sunrise,
each day comes;

sunset,
each day goes.

Have you looked for me?
I was there.

Did you hear my voice?
I spoke to you.

Did you feel my arms around you?
They were there.

I walked every step with you that day.
I heard you cry. I saw your tears but you never
turned my way. You never cried out for me but
I was there and I brought you through.

Trust me,
I was there.

Trust me;
I am here with you now.

I won't let you fall, I love you.
You are my life; I will never let you fall.

Father God

A magnificent life in Christ is one spent not in doing, but in *being.*

Father God

Call on me!

As surely as the spring rains,

I will come;

as surely as the spring rains,

I will come!

Father God

Sickness, pain, and disease
are not from me.

They are abhorrent to me.

My son went to the cross to do away
with all physical and mental suffering.

The stripes He bore on His body were carried and endured for you.

You are free from all maladies;
they do not belong to you.

My church is suffering;
my people are in great bondage to disease.

Why is this? Do you not know that

He gladly and joyously endured the curse for you?

Arise; wake up to what is yours!

Satan has closed your eyes to the truth;
you have been set free from sickness.

Take what has been freely given;
do not let the sacrifice
of my son be in vain.

Father God

You do not need to worry.

I am right beside you.

I know the end from the beginning.

Everything is in My hands.

Father God

So often my children pass me by;
so often they go right by and never turn to me.

I am right here.
Can they not feel me?

I am calling their name.
Can they not see?

I know them.

I know what they are going through
but they do not stop,
they do not listen,
they do not seek me.

My heart breaks for them.
I shout,

I cry out to them but they hear not.
They wander aimlessly through life,
struggling to find happiness when all the time I,
their true happiness,
am right beside them.

If only they would stop,
if only they would pray,

I would answer.

Father God

I have brought you to the edge

of the

alter

and the

cross;

embrace them both

for without them

you will never find me.

Father God

Great is my faithfulness to all who sorrow.
Great is my compassion and mercy
to all those who weep.

Call my name and I will answer;
I will lift you into my arms
and hold you there until the dawn.

Father God

All my creation must die;
nothing will survive forever.
For everything there is that season
of birth, growth, and death.

Why do my children fear the end of life so?
I see the futile efforts so many use to prolong life;
to try to maintain physical beauty and vigor.

Death has to come;
without death there can be no life.
Physical existence is but the precursor of life;
eternal life spent with me.
Why do I show you the sunset?
Why do I give you such beauty that your heart cannot contain it?
It is to give you glimpses of things to come;
to prepare your souls for life after death.

Physical death is a release to the eternal.
Eternal joy, peace, rest, love, happiness;
total goodness.   Why fear the transition?
Why prolong the worldly suffering?
Come, spend eternity with me;
every earthly prayer you have ever prayed
will be fulfilled with me forever.

Father God

Do not weep for your loved one.

They have come to a place of

eternal sunrise;
of eternal light.

Rejoice that all you have ever wished

for them will come to pass;

forever loved,

forever joyful.

Father God

My children,

I am the way, the truth, and the life.

Through me you have all things.

My desire is to bless you,

to fill your heart with heavenly love,

to see all of your needs met.

Believe this, believe in me;

that I can and will give you the

desires of your hearts.

Cling to me as a child;

trust me to do the right thing.

Release all of your burdens

onto me and I will

restore and rebuild.

Father God

I love you, you are mine.

My handprint is upon you.
You belong to me;
no one else can claim you.

You look like me,
you speak my words,
you have my heart.
My spirit lives and
breathes inside you.

You are glorious in my sight;
all of heaven and earth rejoice in you.
Everything I have is yours.
I have made all things for you,
for your pleasure.

Rejoice that your Father loves you!
Shout to the heavens that your Father God
adores you and has made
all things possible!

Father God

Lean on me.

Rest in me at all times.
Allow me to take you in my arms,
to hold you and protect you
from all trouble.

I am a God who restores.

No matter what has happened
in your life up to this point;
I will rebuild the fallen walls,
I will mend your broken heart.

Your dreams will once again be my dreams,
and my dreams for you will come to pass.

You cannot find your own way;
mine is the only path.

Father God

Absolute and total healing depends on you.

I am ready and eager to heal.

Will you come to me in faith?

*Will you abandon all that you are to me
so that I can perform the miracle you need?*

Why would I withhold your healing?

Absolute faith requires absolute trust.

Confidence in my ability and desire to heal is essential.

Find your faith and trust in my word.

How can you trust me when you do not know me?

That is my heart's desire; to free you from all sickness.

Step out of the way,

trust me to restore and rebuild.

Father God

Beauty is in you.

Beauty surrounds you.

Beauty walks with you.

You are the manifestation of me.

Father God

You are my child.

Every created being on earth is my child.

Every color, ethnicity, nationality;

you are all the same in my eyes.

I love you each as a tender shoot of new grass,

as a budding leaf in the spring.

Such is the

promise of

renewed life.

Children are a gift to me.

Each one of you is unique.

Each one a representation

of goodness, of love,

of awesome potential for greatness.

Children are the carriers of my genetic code.

Each one has inside of them everything

they will need for life;

a life filled with abundance.

Each child conceived has a place in my heart;

precious in my sight is each

child of God.

Father God

The hope
that sustains
is that the dawn
will bring a
glimpse of heaven.
Father God

Who is the Holy Spirit; the third person of the Trinity? Several years ago, I attended a church service in which the speaker addressed the subject. He ended by saying that if we listen closely, we can hear that "still, small voice" speaking to us. He said we need to hear a fresh word from the Holy Spirit every day, just as Fresh Manna sustained the Israelites as they wandered the desert.

I wanted to hear God's voice, so I started asking and listening. As I sat with paper and pencil, thoughts came into my mind—words so clearly not from me; words of wisdom and encouragement; beautiful, godly words. I have recorded every word that has come to my spirit from God's Spirit. I have put a portion of these words into this book, as they are truly meant for God's church today. The Holy Spirit is in and around every believer, and He always speaks to those who will listen.

"However, when He, the Spirit of truth, has come, He will guide you into all truth; for He will not speak on His own authority, but whatever He hears He will speak; and He will tell you things to come" (John 16:13).

Kay Bonnell is currently a substitute teacher and artist. Her website, freshmannafromgod.com, shows many additional "love letters" and a number of her prints that have been made into greeting cards. She and her husband live in Mount Pleasant, Michigan.

U.S. $16.95

ISBN 978-1-4908-2300-

9 781490 823003

WestBow
PRESS
A DIVISION OF THOMAS NELSON
& ZONDERVAN

MY LEAF

BOOK ONE

Written and Illustrated by

Maryam K Muhammad, MPH